QUILTING
FOR FUN!

by Dana Meachen Rau

Content Adviser: Lynn Kough, Past President, The National Quilting Association, Inc., Columbus, Ohio
Reading Adviser: Frances J. Bonacci, Ed.D., Reading Specialist, Cambridge, Massachusetts

Compass Point Books ◈ Minneapolis, Minnesota

Compass Point Books
151 Good Counsel Drive
P.O. Box 669
Mankato, MN 56002-0669

This book was manufactured with paper containing at least 10 percent post-consumer waste.

Photographs ©: Bob Daemmrich/The Image Works, cover; Karon Dubke/Capstone Press, back cover, 11 (right), 22–23, 25, 27, 28-29, 31, 32–33; Elizabeth Whiting & Associates/Alamy, 4; D. Hurst/Alamy, 5, 13 (bottom right); Mary Evans Picture Library, 6; Historical Picture Archive/Corbis, 7; Don Despain/www.rekindlephotos.com/Alamy, 8 (bottom); N Joy Neish/Shutterstock, 8–9; Stacey Lynn Brown/Shutterstock, 10–11; Judith Collins/Alamy, 12 (top); Yunus Arakon/iStockphoto, 12 (middle); Robert W. Ginn/Alamy, 12 (bottom); Norma Cornes/iStockphoto, 13 (top right); Tomas Loutocky/Shutterstock, 13 (top left); Jaimie Duplass/Shutterstock, 13 (middle right); Birute Vijeikiene/Shutterstock, 13 (bottom left); Index Stock Imagery/photolibrary, 14–15 (top); Kristian Peetz/Shutterstock, 14–15 (bottom); fotosav/Shutterstock, 16; Rafa Irusta/Shutterstock, 17 (right); Liv friis-larsen/Shutterstock, 19; Virginia Gossman/Shutterstock, 20 (bottom); Christina Richards/iStockphoto, 20–21; Joan Kimball/iStockphoto, 34; Doug Wilson/Alamy, 35; Ted Streshinsky/Corbis, 36 (bottom); Ilene MacDonald/Alamy, 36–37; Stan Rohrer/iStockphoto, 38 (bottom), 47; Hisham Ibrahim/Photov.com/Alamy, 38–39; Dana Meachen Rau, 41; Hulton Archive/Getty Images, 42 (left); North Wind Picture Archives/Alamy, 42 (bottom); World History Archive/Alamy, 42 (right); Library of Congress, 43 (left), 44; Lori Martin/Shutterstock, 43 (right); Patricia Nelson/iStockphoto, 45 (left); Eileen Hart/iStockphoto, 45 (right).

Acknowledgement: Thanks to Chris Lell and Hilary Wacholz for their help with and enthusiasm for this book.

Editor: Brenda Haugen
Page Production: The Design Lab
Photo Researcher: Robert McConnell
Illustrator: Ashlee Suker
Art Director: LuAnn Ascheman-Adams
Creative Director: Keith Griffin
Editorial Director: Nick Healy
Managing Editor: Catherine Neitge

Library of Congress Cataloging-in-Publication Data
Rau, Dana Meachen, 1971–
  Quilting for fun! / by Dana Meachen Rau.
      p. cm. — (For fun)
  Includes index.
  ISBN 978-0-7565-3860-6 (library binding)
1. Quilting—Juvenile literature. I. Title. II. Series.
  TT835.R37 2008
  746.46'041—dc22   2008008274

Visit Compass Point Books on the Internet at *www.compasspointbooks.com*
or e-mail your request to *custserv@compasspointbooks.com*

Table of Contents

The Basics

Doing It

People, Places, and Fun

Note: In this book, there are two kinds of vocabulary words. Quilting Words to Know are words specific to quilting. They are defined on page 46. Other Words to Know are helpful words that are not related only to quilting. They are defined on page 47.

For Beds and for Beauty

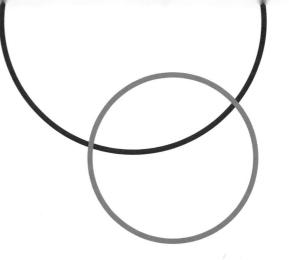

Nothing is cozier than a soft quilt on a cold day. Quilts have been keeping people warm for centuries. But they are not just for warmth. People make quilts to be beautiful, too. In fact, some quilts are never used as blankets. They are hung on walls as artwork.

Most quilts are made of three layers. The top layer can be decorated with different fabrics. The middle layer is the insulation that keeps you warm. The bottom layer, which is called the backing, is another piece of fabric.

The layers' edges are covered with binding to make them stronger and protect the edges of the quilt. The quilt's layers are held together with quilting stitches that are sewn through all three layers with thread.

Do you want to be a quilter? All you need are some basic sewing skills and some colorful ideas, and you are ready to go.

How Does a Quilt Keep You Warm?

A quilt is kind of like a house. You stay warm in a house because it has an outside wall, an inside wall, and a layer of insulation in between.

The insulation in a quilt is not made of the same stuff as the insulation in a house. But it serves the same purpose. The inside layer between two fabrics keeps out the cold.

Quilts Through the Ages

The process of piecing fabric together and decorating it with sewn designs began in ancient cultures of the Middle East and Asia. Quilted objects have been found in tombs and shown on sculptures of people who lived thousands of years ago.

When knights from Europe traveled to the Middle East to fight in the Crusades in the 12th century, they saw this way of sewing. They brought quilted items with them when they returned home. People in Europe and throughout the world began quilting clothing. They also quilted bed covers to keep them warm during cold winter nights.

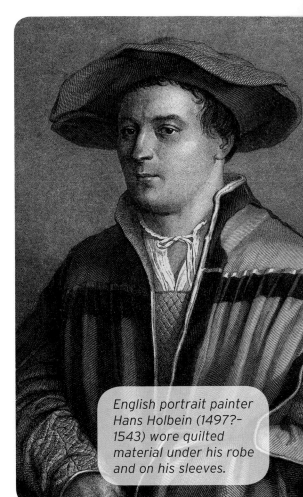

English portrait painter Hans Holbein (1497?-1543) wore quilted material under his robe and on his sleeves.

All sorts of people made quilts. Queens sewed pieces for the castles. Peasants used scraps of fabric to make quilts for their families.

When settlers came to America from Europe in the 1600s, they brought some quilt-making traditions with them. The piecework-type quilt developed quickly in America. In the mid-1800s, factories began making fabrics in large amounts and many varieties. More types of fabric were now available to more people.

Not as many quilts were made in the early 1900s, but quilting became popular again in the 1970s. In 1976, the United States celebrated its bicentennial, and many people became interested in their history. Quilting was a part of that history. Soon people made quilts as art, moving them off the bed and onto the walls to be admired. Today quilters gather in groups or work alone to create their art.

Finding Clues to the Past

Many quilts from history have not survived. So how do we know they existed? Long ago, when someone died, people would make an inventory, or list, of their household items. Quilts often were mentioned on these lists.

Patterns With Fabric and Thread

Every quilt looks different. Each is handmade with different patterns, designs, or colors. But, in general, there are three ways to create the top of a quilt.

A piecework quilt is made of different pieces of fabric stitched together. The shapes are usually squares, triangles, or rectangles. These shapes are organized into a pattern block. The blocks are repeated and organized into a larger pattern to create the quilt top.

Piecework quilt

Appliqué quilt

An appliqué quilt also is made of different fabrics. But instead of joining small pieces together, a piece of fabric is cut into the desired shape and sewn onto a background fabric. The background pieces are joined to make the quilt top.

A whole cloth quilt top is made from one fabric. It is decorated with stitched patterns. Quilting is the process of making designs with thread while stitching through the layers of the quilt to hold it together. Piecework quilts and appliqué quilts are usually quilted with designs, too.

Lots of Blocks

Some pattern blocks have been used for hundreds of years. The log cabin block is made of strips that surround a center square. The center square is often red to symbolize the fireplace of a welcoming home.

The Soft Stuff

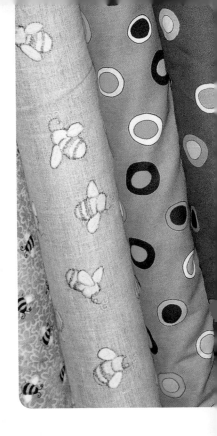

Fabric: Quilting stores have many fabrics to choose from. Fabrics come in solid colors, small prints, large prints, and stripes. They also come in every color. Cotton fabric is the best choice for quilts. You can mix any colors or patterns you wish, as long as you are happy with the way they look together.

All fabric has a right side and a wrong side. For printed fabrics, the right side is the side with the design. The wrong side is the back of the fabric that you will not see. Keep these sides in mind as you follow sewing instructions for your quilting projects.

Fabric is sold by the yard or portions of a yard, such as one-quarter or one-third. Sometimes you can buy fabric in smaller, prepackaged pieces, since you often don't need big pieces. You also will need a larger single piece or several pieces joined together for the back of the quilt.

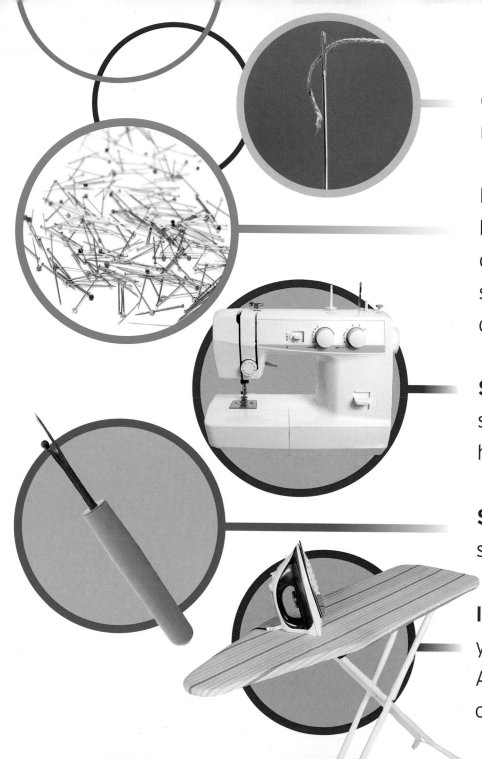

Needle: If you are sewing by hand or quilting designs onto your quilt, you will need a needle.

Pins: Pins hold your fabrics together before you sew them. Choose pins with colorful round heads. They are easier to spot on your work and on the floor if you drop them.

Sewing machine: An adult will be able to show you how to thread the machine and how to safely sew with it.

Seam ripper: This tool can easily take out sewing mistakes.

Iron and ironing board: You will press your fabric flat as you make your quilt. Ask an adult to help you because an iron can cause serious burns.

Simple Stitches

If you are making a piecework quilt, your main sewing task will be joining pieces of fabric together. The line of sewing that joins two fabrics is called the seam. You can use a sewing machine, or you can sew by hand. A sewing machine is faster. Sewing by hand takes longer, but you can take your sewing with you wherever you go.

You must master various stitches in order to make quilted designs and to connect the three layers. Here are some basic sewing stitches.

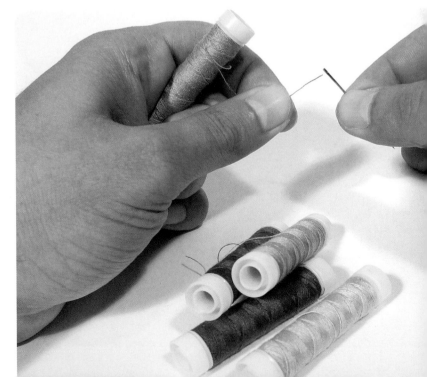

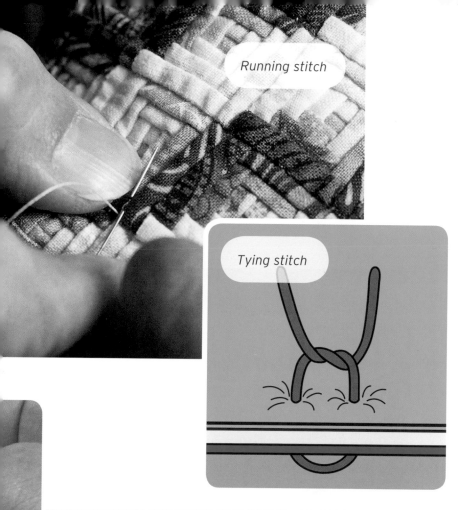

Running stitch

Tying stitch

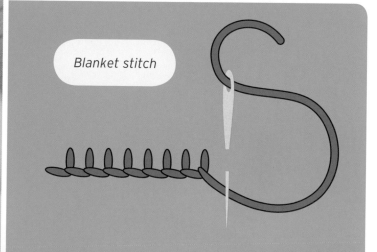

Blanket stitch

Running stitch: You will use this stitch to hold together fabric for a piecework quilt or to create quilted designs. To create a running stitch, push the needle down through the fabric and then back up through the fabric.

Tying stitch: This stitch is a simple way to join layers of fabric. Starting on the quilt top, push the needle down through all the layers. Then push the needle back up near the same hole. Cut the end of the thread, and tie the two ends into a knot.

Blanket stitch: This stitch makes a fancy edge in appliqué quilts. Push the needle down. Then push the needle back up again at the edge of the appliqué piece, looping the surface thread around the needle as it comes up.

Looking for Inspiration

You want to make a quilt, but you might not know where to start. Look through quilting books, magazines, or Internet sites. They are filled with pictures and patterns to give you ideas.

You might be inspired in other places. If you walk outside, you might notice the colors of flowers in a garden. You could make a quilt to match your favorite colors in your room.

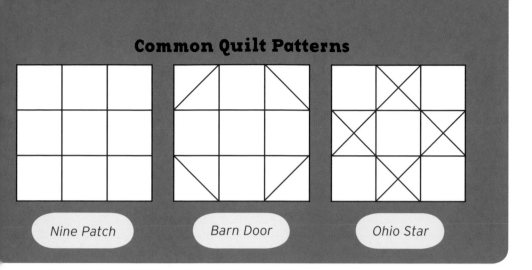

Common Quilt Patterns

Nine Patch

Barn Door

Ohio Star

Drawing your ideas is a good way to plan your quilt. Get a piece of graph paper and some colored pencils. Try different layouts of squares in different colors. Try using triangles together to make diamond shapes. Think of what colors look good in certain patterns. Keep experimenting with colors and shapes until you have created your pattern block. Then see how grouping these pattern blocks together will look.

You also can cut out squares and triangles from colored construction paper. Move them around on a table, and see all the designs you can make.

You now have your pattern!

Making the Lines Just Right

Math plays a big part in quilting. Each of your measurements has to be accurate, or your blocks may not fit together well.

Decide about how big you want your quilt. If you want a small quilt 36 inches (91.4 centimeters) wide, and your pattern has three blocks across, then each block is 12 inches (30.5 cm) wide. And if your block is made up of three squares across, then each square is 4 inches (10.2 cm) wide. If you want a border on your quilt, you have to add in those measurements, too.

You will draw lines on the wrong side of your fabric so you know where to cut out your squares. But wait before you cut. If you need a 4-inch (10.2-cm) square on your finished quilt, you do not want to cut out a 4-inch (10.2-cm) square from the fabric. You need some extra fabric on all sides for your seams. You will be sewing about 1/4 inch (6 millimeters) in on the edges of the fabric. So to get a 4-inch (10.2-cm) square for your finished quilt, you will cut out a 4 1/2-inch (11.4-cm) square.

To make sure all your fabric squares are the same size, you should make a template from plastic or heavy cardboard. Make the template the size your squares should be, and trace around it on the fabric. Place a piece of fine-grade sandpaper under your fabric as you are drawing. This will help keep the fabric from stretching or moving as you draw lines around the template.

You can draw in your sewing lines—1/4 inch (6 mm) in from each side—so you have a square within your square. Drawing these lines now will make sewing easier later.

Wash First!

Many quilters will advise you to wash, dry, and iron all of your fabrics before you cut them. Then if you ever need to wash your finished quilt, you don't have to worry that some fabrics will shrink and others will not.

Working Bit by Bit

Putting a quilt together is done in small steps. Always refer to your pattern so you know which pieces should be joined. It can get confusing if you don't have your plan next to you.

You will make one block at a time. Start by pinning one square to the next, right sides together, and sewing them along the seam line. Then keep adding pieces until you have your block. Iron the seams flat after each addition.

A quilter uses a thimble to protect her finger as she pushes the needle through the fabric.

When your blocks are done, start sewing the blocks together. Always try to make your seams line up straight. With a lot of patience and working bit by bit, soon your quilt top will be done.

Next layer the back fabric, batting, and quilt top. After your three layers are in place, you can join the layers together using tying stitches or with quilted designs. (Making a quilt border is explained on pages 24–25.) You can further embellish your quilt with beads, buttons, or appliqué. You are the artist. Your quilt can be whatever you wish.

Lots of Room

Making a quilt can take many hours, days, or even weeks. Find a place in your home where you can safely spread out your project until you finish it.

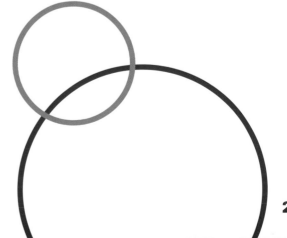

Part 1: The Quilt Top

This project will help you piece together piecework squares. Your finished quilt will be about 20 inches x 20 inches (50.8 cm x 50.8 cm).

1. Place one square of fabric A on top of one square of fabric B, right sides together. Pin them together down one side of the square 1/4 inch (6 mm) in from the edge. Sew along this line of pins. Open the squares and iron them flat. You now have a rectangle shape. Repeat seven more times on the rest of the squares to make a total of eight rectangles.

2. Place one rectangle on top of another, right sides together, so that the fabrics alternate in colors. Pin them together across one of

Materials

- 8 squares of fabric A, 5 1/2 inches x 5 1/2 inches (14 cm x 14 cm)
- 8 squares of fabric B, 5 1/2 inches x 5 1/2 inches (14 cm x 14 cm)
- Thread
- Pins
- Iron and ironing board
- Sewing machine

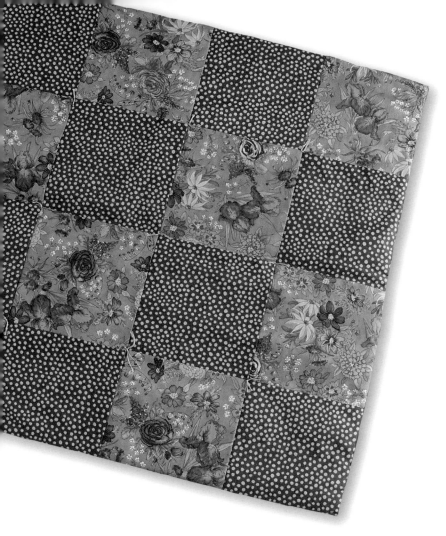

3. Place one block on top of another, right sides together, so that the fabrics alternate in color. Pin them together along the right side 1/4 inch (6 mm) in from the edge. Sew along this line of pins. Open the blocks, and iron them flat. You will have a checkerboard rectangle. Repeat one more time on the rest of the blocks. You will have a total of two rectangles.

4. Place one rectangle on top of the other, right sides together, so that the fabrics alternate in color. Pin them together along the top side 1/4 inch (6 mm) in from the edge. Sew along this line of pins. Open and iron it flat. You now have a checkerboard square—the top of your checkerboard quilt.

the long sides 1/4 inch (6 mm) in from the edge. Sew along this line of pins. Open the rectangles, and iron them flat. You now have a checkerboard block. Repeat three more times on the rest of the rectangles to make a total of four blocks.

Part 2: Putting It Together

1. Lay the piece of batting flat on a table or the floor. Center your quilt top, right side up, on top of the batting. Pin the two layers together. Cut the batting to the same size as your quilt top.

2. Lay the piece of fabric C (the quilt back), wrong side up, flat on the table. Center the quilt top and batting on fabric C. Pin the layers together. Cut the fabric C about 2 inches (5 cm) larger than your quilt top and batting all around.

Materials

- Fabric C for quilt back, 24 inches x 24 inches (61 cm x 61 cm)
- Batting, 22 inches x 22 inches (56 cm x 56 cm)
- Thread
- Pins
- Sewing machine

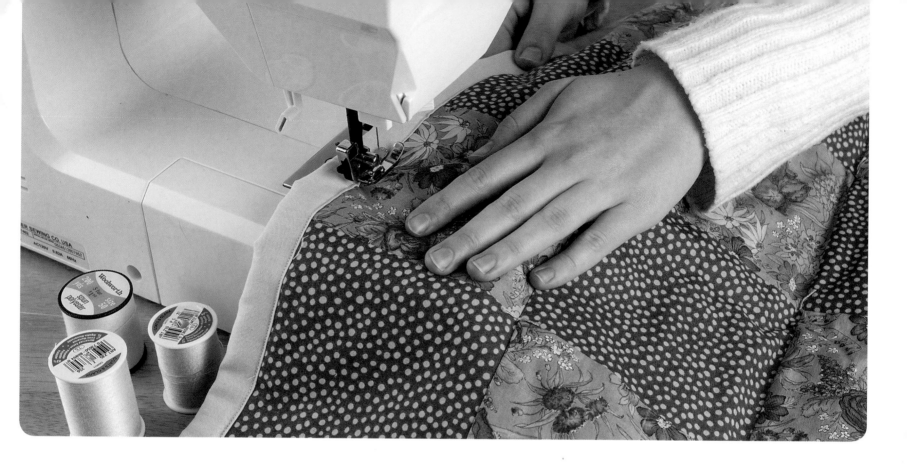

3. Along the top edge, fold over the rough edge of fabric C. Then fold it over again so it overlaps the quilt top. Pin it down all along the edge. Sew it across the top, near the inside edge of the folded fabric. Make sure the stitches go through all the layers.

4. Repeat step 3 along the bottom, then the two sides. Make tying stitches at the corners of each square to hold the three layers together.

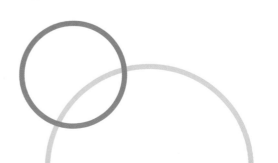

Triangle Sachet

Are you ready to make piecework triangles? This project will help show you how.

- 2 squares of fabric A, 5 inches x 5 inches (12.7 cm x 12.7 cm)
- 2 squares of fabric B, 5 inches x 5 inches (12.7 cm x 12.7 cm)
- Pencil
- Ruler
- 15-inch (38-cm) piece of ribbon
- Dried lavender or potpourri crushed into small bits
- Thread
- Pins
- Sewing machine
- Iron and ironing board

1. Place one square of fabric A on top of one square of fabric B, right sides together. With a pencil and ruler, draw a diagonal line from one corner to the other. Pin the squares together across this diagonal line.

2. Sew from one corner to the other along the diagonal line. Take out the pins. Open the square to reveal a square made up of two triangles. Iron the square flat. Cut off the extra

fabric from the back of the square. Repeat steps 1 and 2 with the other two squares. Now you have two "triangle" squares.

3. Place the "triangle" squares right sides together so the fabrics alternate. Sew 1/4 inch (6 mm) in from the edge along three sides, leaving the top open.

4. Turn your "pocket" inside out so the right sides are now on the outside. Fold in the rough edges of fabric on the open end. Iron the pocket and the folded edges flat. Fill this pocket with the lavender.

5. Tuck in the ribbon ends in the top left corner so that you have formed a loop. Pin the top closed. Sew along the top to close the end and to hold the ribbon in place. Sew along the other sides, too, so that all the edges match.

6. Hang your sachet on a doorknob or a hanger, or place it in a drawer to keep your clothes smelling nice.

Free-form Quilted Wall Hanging

1. Choose a fabric for your quilt top that has a pattern. Fabric with a large pattern, such as flowers or spots, works well for this project.

2. Create a small "quilt" by following the directions for putting a quilt top, batting, and backing together on pages 24–25 (but do not use tying stitches to hold

Materials

- Fabric A (printed fabric for the quilt top), 12 inches x 16 inches (30.5 cm x 40.6 cm)
- Batting, 12 inches x 16 inches (30.5 cm x 40.6 cm)
- Fabric B (for quilt back), 15 inches x 19 inches (38 cm x 48.3 cm)
- Thread
- Pins
- Sewing machine
- 2 small plastic rings

3. You will hold the three layers together by quilting them with thread. Use thread that matches the colors of the designs on your top fabric. Outline the images on the fabric by hand sewing with a running stitch or sewing slowly with a sewing machine. Switch thread colors if needed as you trace around different images. Add extra lines or shapes on the quilt top if you wish. If you are hand sewing, tie your knots in the back so they do not show.

the layers together). Your quilt top will be the printed fabric. Make sure to leave the three layers securely pinned together.

4. On the back of your quilt, sew the small rings in the top two corners for hanging.

Quilted Purse

1. Lay out the piece of fabric A right side up. With a ruler and pencil, draw diagonal lines evenly spaced from side to side over the whole fabric. Then draw diagonal lines in the other direction until you have a diamond pattern covering the whole piece.

2. Lay out the piece of fabric B wrong side up on the table. Place the batting on top of fabric B. Place fabric A on top of the batting, right side up. All three layers should be lined up on the long sides. On both short sides, fabric B should extend about 2 inches (5 cm). Pin the three layers together.

Materials

- Fabric A (outside of purse), 12 inches x 22 inches (30.5 cm x 56 cm)
- Fabric B (inside of purse), 12 inches x 26 inches (30.5 cm x 66 cm)
- Thin cotton batting, 12 inches x 22 inches (30.5 cm x 56 cm)
- 1-inch (2.5-cm) wide ribbon (long enough to be a handle)
- Ruler
- Pencil
- Thread
- Pins
- Sewing machine

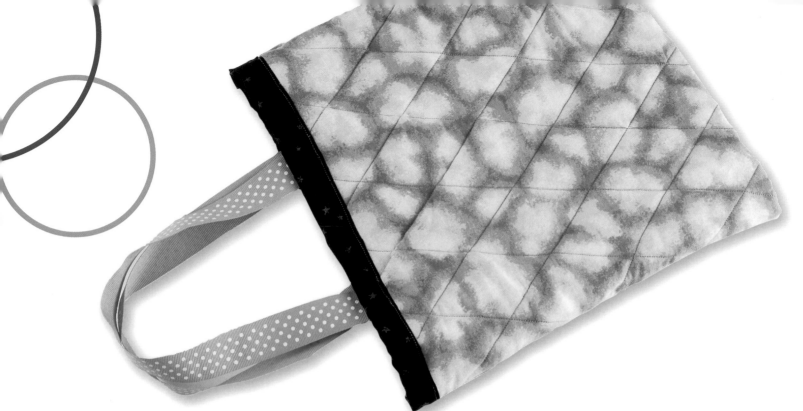

3. Using a sewing machine, sew along all the diagonal lines through all three layers of fabric. Start with the middle lines. Then jump around a bit from line to line to be sure the layers connect evenly without too much bunching together.

4. Finish the short sides by folding the inside fabric over the edges as described on page 25.

5. Fold the piece in half horizontally with the inside fabric facing out. Pin the two sides closed, and sew along the sides through all layers. Using a running stitch, sew the ribbons onto the top edges of each side as handles.

6. Turn the bag so the correct fabric is facing out.

Happy Cat Face

This project will help you learn the quilting technique appliqué. When you're done making this appliquéd piece, you can sew it onto a pillow or add it to a larger quilt.

1. Cut a simple cat face shape from the orange felt.

2. Cut a large circle (cheeks) from the white felt. Lay it on the cat face, and pin it in place. Blanket stitch this piece down with matching thread.

3. Cut two small ovals (eyes) from the yellow felt. Lay them on the face, and pin them in place. Blanket stitch these pieces down with matching thread.

Materials

- Orange felt
- White felt
- Yellow felt
- Pink felt
- Needle
- Thread (white, yellow, pink, and black)
- Scissors

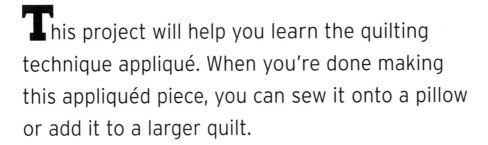

4. Cut three triangles (two for ears and one for nose) from the pink felt. Lay them on the cat face, and pin them in place. Blanket stitch these pieces down with matching thread.

5. With black thread knotted in the back, sew a few overlapping stitches inside each eye to make the pupil.

6. With black thread knotted in the back, use a running stitch to sew a line down from the nose and off to each side to make a mouth.

Fabric on Display

Quilts have always been considered beautiful. However, through history they have mainly been used as clothing or bedcovers. But in 1971, the Whitney

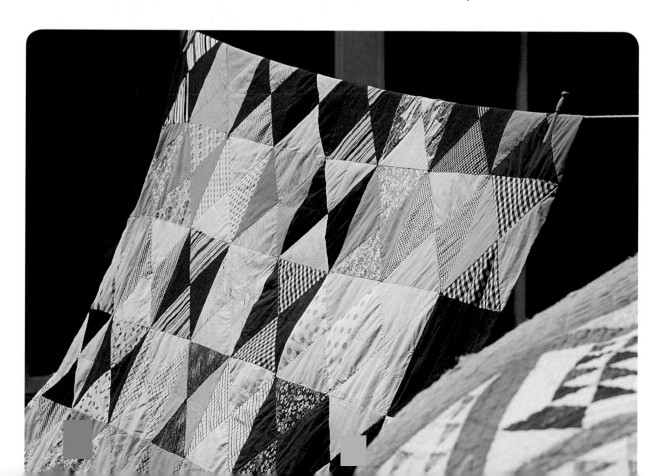

Museum of American Art displayed quilts on its walls. Here they were admired in the same way as paintings were. People started to think of quilts as art.

Artists began experimenting with fabric and thread as a medium. The fabric was like paint on a canvas. Artists could use many colors of fabric or even dye their own. Like collage, artists could piece their fabrics together in interesting ways. Portraits, landscapes, or modern-day designs could be created using the techniques of piecework, appliqué, and quilting. Artists also could break the rules to create new and unique ways of using fabric and thread.

Today many museums display quilts in special exhibits. Some museums are devoted just to quilts and other fabric arts.

The Quilt Museum in Lancaster, Pennsylvania

Famous Quilter

Nancy Crow is a famous quilt artist. Her works of art have been shown at museums and galleries around the world.

Different Quilts in Different Places

While many quilters follow similar patterns, different traditions have developed among different people.

Hawaiian quilts: Appliqué quilts are a tradition in Hawaii. The background quilt top is usually just one color. The appliqué is sewn onto the quilt top with many delicate stitches. The quilt often has designs based on the nature of Hawaii, such as leaves, flowers, or pineapples.

Hawaiian quilt

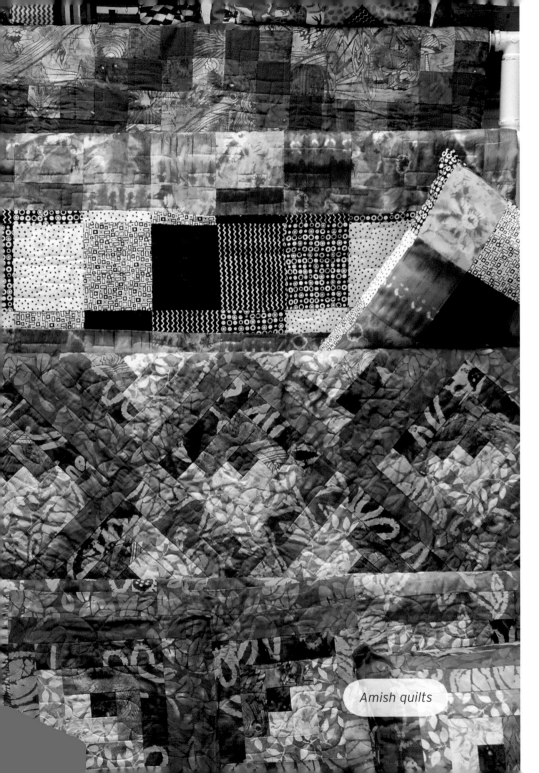

Amish quilts

Hmong story cloths: The Hmong people of Southeast Asia have created beautiful designs and pictures with thread for thousands of years. One type of Hmong art is the story cloth. It often is stitched with bright thread on a dark background. These cloths show daily life or stories about the history of the Hmong people.

Amish quilts: The Amish people live simply. They don't have cars, phones, or electricity. Their quilts are also simple but bold. They often use black as well as bright, solid colors and patterns. They usually make strict piecework designs.

A Quilt to Remember

Memory quilts are made to remember loved ones who have died. A quilter might make a quilt in the loved one's favorite colors or include pictures of the person transferred onto fabric. Quilters also might use scraps of the loved one's clothing pieced together.

The largest quilt in the world is a memory quilt. The AIDS Memorial Quilt was created by people who lost loved ones to AIDS.

A memory quilt may include a loved one's favorite colors.

The AIDS Memorial Quilt on display in Washington, D.C.

The quilt was first displayed in 1987. People could view it on the National Mall in Washington, D.C. It has been on display and on tour many times since then. It also has grown in size. The quilt has more than 46,000 panels, 3 feet x 6 feet (91 cm x 183 cm) each, in remembrance of 91,000 people.

The AIDS Memorial Quilt is the largest community art project in the world. The money collected when the quilt goes on tour helps increase awareness of HIV and AIDS. It also funds educational programs about the prevention of HIV infection as well as helping those who suffer with the disease.

Not Just Fabric

The AIDS Memorial Quilt is made of many types of fabric. The quilt also includes items that help people remember their loved ones. Some panels have flip-flops, car keys, and even toys.

Helping Others With Quilts

Anne Sousa, a quilter from Newington, Connecticut, had an idea. She knew of a shelter for women and children. The shelter needed quilts for its many beds. Sousa was part of a quilting guild, or group. She knew that she and her fellow quilters could create 16 quilts in five months to give to the shelter.

"These women sew for the love of sewing and to show their love and concern," Sousa said of her guild. The guild met about once a month. Members brought their sewing machines and current projects. They shared the work. When someone finished a quilt top, another person helped make the borders or tied the quilt together. One person cut pieces for the next person to sew. Together they solved quilting problems and learned from each other.

You can start your own quilting guild.

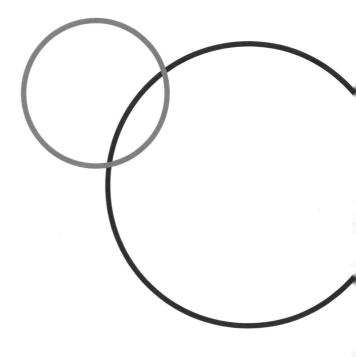

They made some of the quilts in soothing colors, such as blues and purples. They made some quilts in kid-friendly fabrics, with princesses and frogs. The quilts sent a comforting message to the people at the shelter. The quilts showed that someone cared for them. The guild had used their time to make something special for people at the shelter without expecting anything in return.

You can create a quilting guild of your own. Find some friends who share your excitement about quilting, and make a quilt together. Then you can give that quilt to someone as a gift.

What Happened When?

1100   1200   1300   1700   1800

14th century
Quilting frames are invented to help people make large bedcovers.

1793 Eli Whitney invents the cotton gin, which makes the processing of cotton easier.

1189 Crusaders see quilting in the Middle East and bring the idea to Europe.

1700s Americans make piecework quilt tops.

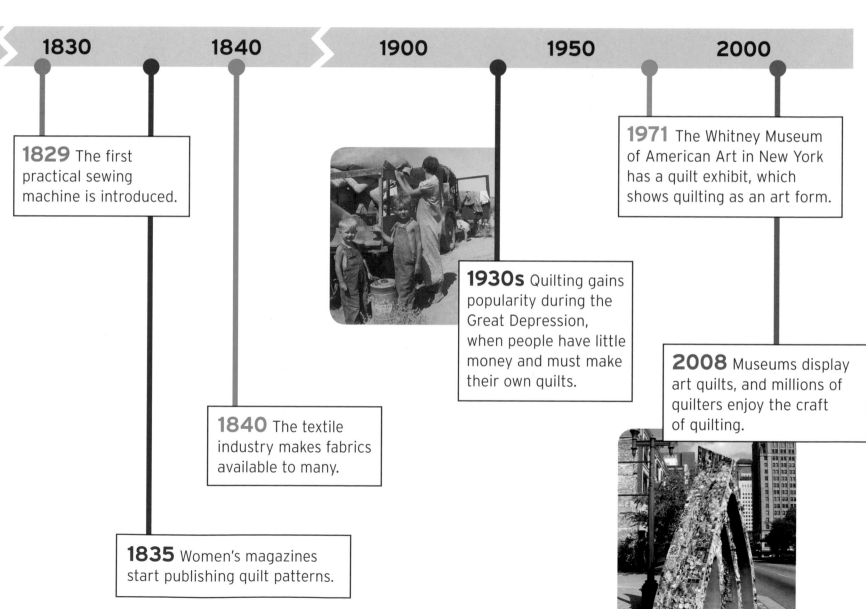

1830   **1840**   **1900**   **1950**   **2000**

1829 The first practical sewing machine is introduced.

1971 The Whitney Museum of American Art in New York has a quilt exhibit, which shows quilting as an art form.

1930s Quilting gains popularity during the Great Depression, when people have little money and must make their own quilts.

2008 Museums display art quilts, and millions of quilters enjoy the craft of quilting.

1840 The textile industry makes fabrics available to many.

1835 Women's magazines start publishing quilt patterns.

Fun Quilting Facts

Groups of women used to gather at friends' homes, where quilts were set up on large frames. Together they worked on stitching the quilts. They also used the time to chat and enjoy being with friends. These gatherings were called quilting bees.

Not many quilts made for Civil War soldiers exist today. The soldiers who died on the battlefield were often buried in the quilts people had made for them.

Knights fighting in the Crusades wore quilted shirts under their armor for comfort and warmth.

Mary, Queen of Scots (1542–1587), was an expert quilter. She decorated wall hangings, bedcovers, and other castle linens.

The Hard Parts

Right triangle and ruler: You will be drawing shapes with 90-degree angles. A right triangle tool will help you do this. Office supply stores sell plastic right triangles that also act as rulers. A clear or pastel plastic tool works the best. When you place it over the fabric, you can still see the design underneath.

Scissors: Fabric scissors are different from paper scissors. Fabric scissors are much sharper. Be careful when you use them.

Pencils, chalk, or markers: You will make lines on your fabric to show you where to cut or sew. A regular pencil or marker can work, but the marks may not wash out of your fabric. Quilting stores sell special tools for making marks on fabric.

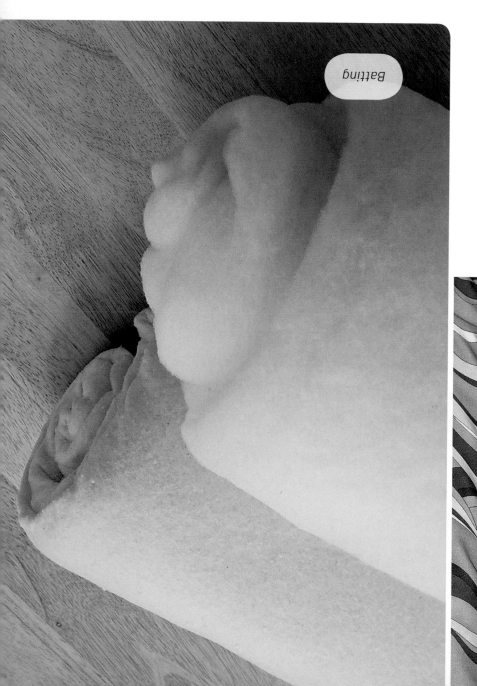

Batting

Batting: Batting, the insulation layer, is usually prepackaged. However, sometimes you can buy it by the yard.

Thread: All-purpose thread works well for piecework and appliqué quilts, but there are special threads made for hand or machine quilting. It is best to choose a thread color that matches your fabrics.